I0417681

Dedication

This book is dedicated to my wife, Michelle Canolo, who inspired me to compile these quotations' and share it to inspire other people as well.

This is also dedicated to all the people who in one way or another contributed to the success of this endeavor.

Copyright @ 2012 Glen Quilab

All Rights Reserved

Introduction

Surviving in a chaotic, dishonest and generally insensitive society is difficult. Any individual or group seeks to obtain from life what pleasure and freedom from pain that we can. Your own happiness can be turned into sorrow by the misconduct of others surrounding you.

There are many people one influences wherein it can be good or it can be bad. Despite the insistence of evil men that men are evil, there are many good men around and women, too, who can Lift You Up when you are down. You may have been fortunate enough to know some.

Sometimes others seek to crush one down, to make nothing out of one's hopes and dreams, one's future and one, himself. For whatever reason, efforts to improve oneself, to become happier in life, can become the subject of attack. It is sometimes necessary to handle such directly. But there is a long range handling that seldom fails. The real handling of such a situation and such people, the way to defeat them, is to flourish and prosper.

This pocketbook is a collection of inspiring text quotes that held me up when I am down or being pulled down. Hope this will also help you as you journey into this world. Let yourself be a guide and light to others as well while creating chapters in life.

Part 1

Never get discourage when things go beyond your expectation. Always remember that the greatest story in life is not winning, but rising again every time we fall.

Life is so short, so never hold back. Forgive like you have amnesia, believe like a kid, love like crazy, and never regret anything that made you happy.

Life is too ironic to understand fully. It takes sadness to know what happiness is, noise to appreciate silence and a cross to get to paradise.

Sometimes we search so much for the right choices, for the right paths to walk through, for the right time, for the right person and for the right reasons. But life is not about searching for things that can be found. It is about letting the unexpected happen and finding things you never searched for.

Life is too short; grudges are a waste of perfect HAPPINESS. LAUGH when you can, APOLOGIZE when you should and let go of what you can't change. LOVE deeply and FORGIVE quickly. Take chances... give everything and have no regrets. LIFE is too short to be UNHAPPY; you have to take the good with the bad. SMILE when you're sad. LOVE what you got and always remember what you had. Always FORGIVE but never forget. LEARN from your mistakes but never REGRET. People change, and things go wrong, but always remember... LIFE goes on.

Don't just neglect an effort of a person to keep in touch. People get tired; it's not all the time that they hold on...

When life gets difficult, when task becomes tiring, when you're about to give up... Always remember that the snail got to Noah's Ark inch by inch to SURVIVE.

Giving up something doesn't mean your WEAK Instead It makes you STRONG to let go of something important to you because LOVE is what makes you complete.

We spend our whole lives telling ourselves everything happens for a reason... when in reality, we just give reasons for everything that happens.

It's hard when you meet the right LOVE at the wrong time but what is more painful is when you have to give up the right LOVE because you have to face the right TIME holding the wrong LOVE.

Never tell yourself, "I am tired". The more you accept that thought... the more exhausted you'll become... but if you tell yourself, "I can do even more"... you'll find that there are no limits to what you accomplish.

Do what makes you happy. LIFE is not based on the money you earn or the success you have achieved, it's all about being HAPPY with who you are with who you loved and who makes your LIFE complete.

A SMILE is the best lighting system of the face... the best cooling system of the head... and the best warming system of the heart.

Friend means trusting yourself with someone who has seen you at your worst and loves you anyway... it means teasing each other and laughing at inside jokes nobody but only the two of you understands... it means feeling safe enough to talk about anything and having patience to work out disagreements... it means counting on someone who sympathizes when you had a bad day, worries about you when you're gone too long... and always welcomes you with open arms.

In LIFE there are times you have to face though decisions, either you make it or you break it, but do remember... whatever way you go – there are no wrong decisions in life, it's for you to make it right.

Someday, we'll forget the pains, which caused the tears and why we cried... we would finally realize that the secret of being free is not revenge but letting go.

No one can go back and make a new beginning, but anyone can start from now and make a happy ending.

When you love someone let them know. You never know what will happen in the next minute.

A perfect start doesn't promise a perfect ending but how you finish is just as important as how you begin... run Life's race with patience and perseverance.

Don't be afraid to take the chances even if it might get you hurt, just be strong and take it, because you might miss that single chance that would change your life and make you really happy.

Silence doesn't always mean yes, it may also mean no but it's better left unsaid.

Anger doesn't always mean hatred; it could just be a means coping.

Laughter doesn't always mean happiness, sometimes it's just a mask.

Tears doesn't always mean sorrow, it may also be an outlet of joy.

Staying away doesn't always mean it's the end, it may also mean the best beginning... and though life is so complicated, it is always beautiful. Live life to the fullest.

Butterflies don't know the color of their wings, but human eyes know how beautiful it is, likewise you don't know how good you are, but others can see you are special.

The best of friendship does not only shows when you're together, it shows when you're apart yet you realized that... despite distance and silence, friendship still...survives.

Sometimes, we find ourselves feeling incomplete. Longing for something we can't explain. And we are caught in the middle of going nowhere. Weird isn't it? But that's the beauty of being human. It's knowing that there is a purpose for each existence and whatever that maybe, it is also the reason why we still wake up breathing each day to discover the missing piece of the puzzle that would make our lives complete.

Rivers don't drink the water they carry; Trees don't eat the fruit they bear; Clouds don't bathe in the rain they produce. We are meant to give, even if we get nothing from it. Measuring life by what others do may disappoint us, but measuring life by what we do makes meaningful.

The worst regret we can have in life is not for the wrong things we did, but for the right things we could have done but we never did.

It is not the presence of someone that brings meaning to LIFE. It's the way that someone touches your heart that gives life a beautiful meaning.

The way you deal with your struggles depends on how you view them. Always remember: there are no hopeless situations, only people who think hopelessly.

No one is rich enough to buy back yesterday. But if have the character to do better things today, you would be the richest one tomorrow.

Sometimes, smiling doesn't means happiness at all... maybe it's just the only way to say "I can manage"... but sometimes smiling is just a way of people to say..."I'm tired of crying.

Never beg people to be against their will... sometimes the gift of goodbyes opens up another door... move on, but never move away.

Life is full of twist and turns. Learn to enjoy the ride no matter how bumpy it is, for in every twist and turn, a blessing is always given in return.

Never be afraid to try something new because life gets boring when you stay within the limits of what you already know. Life is too short to have no fun and yet too precious to waste.

If someone hurts you, don't mind it; because it is the law of nature that the tree that bears the sweetest fruits gets the maximum number of stones.

They say if love becomes painful it's time to let that love go and save you but just keep this in mind: If love is true, pain is never a reason to let go.

Pain of missing friends isn't their absence, but it's when you think of the good times you have shared and you ask yourself: Will those moments ever happen again?

Time is like a river. You cannot touch the same water twice, because the flow that has passed will never pass again... enjoy every moment of life.

Friendship is not choosing the right person, but creating happy moments... it's not how much you love your friends from the start, but how much you value and keep them until the end.

You'll never know how much you need your friends unless you look back along the rope and realize how many knots they have tied to keep you from falling...

Life itself is a challenge that we ought to face. You lose someone, you'll win someone, but if you never give up, you will discover that SACRIFICES have greater rewards.

Deep friendship doesn't depend on how many times we spend time together... how happy we are... it's the time when you never see them... yet keep on believing that friendship will stay forever.

True people are those capable of caring from a distance, far enough to make other people grow but never too far to feel the care within their hearts.

Be strong... never tell yourself, "I am tired". The more you accept that thought... the more exhausted you'll become... but if you tell yourself, I can do even more... you'll find that there are no limits to what you can accomplish.

Don't always say that there is still time, because there's also a painful concept of it's too late.

Sometimes we put too much passion on the biggest dreams and priorities in life that we fail to love the smallest pleasures from simple things... We search so much for the right time, and for the right reasons... but life isn't about searching for the things that can't be found... it is about letting the unexpected happen and finding things you never searched for.

A great life is not about routine but doing something rare. To cherish and not to compare. To forgive and not to blame, to love without counting. Laugh at your mistakes, but learn from them. Joke over your troubles but gather strength from them. Have fun with your difficulties but overcome them.

Don't ever get tired of what's going on with your life because you'll never know the plans and reasons behind it, instead just walk on. From there you'll see the beauty that you've never seen before.

In the silence of your heart, listen to the memory of goodness. What have you done for others is the sweetest song your heart can ever hold.

In the garden of life... If we plant openness we reap intimacy, if we plant patience we reap improvements, if we plant faith we reap miracles.

Whatever makes you happy, do it more often because it will bring lightness to your heart, energy to your body and wonders to your soul.

Sometimes you need to experience everything so that you would learn... there is no easy ways in living life so live it as it is. Cry, Laugh, be Angry, and don't miss the chances that Life is giving you because the most important things are not things at all, most of the time, they are people making your life worth living.

A question that will awaken you:

What is a trash can?

... To a kid, it's just a container for his ugly toys.

... To a student, it is where she keeps her bad test papers.

... To a teenager, it's a basket case for the letters of an ex-lover.

... to a writer, it's where the files of rejected drafts are thrown, but to a street children... it is where they depend on to live.... Give LOVE.

Never take someone for granted. Hold the right person close to your heart because you might wake up one day realizing that you've lost a diamond while you were busy collecting stones.

It's by LOVE that we SERVE. It's by PATIENCE that we UNDERSTAND. It's by TRIALS that we gain WISDOM. It's by SHARING that we become a BLESSING.

Appreciate Life itself even if it's not perfect. Contentment is not a fulfillment of what we wish for, but an appreciation of what we have.

We choose how we see people. When we want to like someone, we can be so tolerant. When we want to be irritated, we focus on their faults. It's not other persons that determine how we feel about them, it's our attitude.

Life is hard... because we see obstacles, not the goals.

Life is painful... because we see the tears, not the smiles.

People are rejected... because we see their faults, not their righteous deeds.

People are weak... because we see their failures, not their success.

It is the way we look at things that makes this world a bit complicated. May we always see what is good in each other that what is not.

When you share yourself with others, life begins to find its meaning. The time you touch the lives of others is the moment you truly live your purpose.

Every sixty seconds you spend angry, upset or mad is a full minute of happiness you'll never get back. Life is too short... break the rules. Forgive quickly, Kiss slowly, Love truly, Laugh uncontrollably... and most importantly, never regret anything that made you smile.

Never get tired of doing little good things for others... oftentimes... those little things occupy the biggest part of their hearts.

One of the finest hours in our life is... when we have done good things to nameless people without expecting them to remember our acts of love and kindness.

The most honorable gifts of goodness are given in secret. It flows from a good heart... A heart that has no need for recognition. A heart that sacrifices without any hint of resentment. A heart that joyfully shares what is hardest to share... our very selves.

As we journey thru the path of life, we must examine our baggage. Are we weighed down by negative thoughts, fear that we don't measure up to some standards, past misdeeds and false lessons? Unload them, it makes our life's journey heavier. Lighten the load, retain only positive thoughts. Forgive, love more and entrust everything to our maker.

Real friendship isn't affected by social status, distance or even time. Real friendship isn't tarnished by money or lack of it or it is enhanced by prestige and success. A real friend will always believe in you, always expect the best in you, and stand his ground in defending you.

To have everything is one of the highest delights of life; to give everything is one of the noblest and most difficult undertakings.

Time is a rare luxury which can never be purchased at any cost. So when someone spends it for you, it defines the depth of care they have with you.

The joy of life comes from the wisdom of counting our blessings and not our troubles... we should focus on what we have and maintain a thankful heart.

It's not how many goals we have reached, but how many lives we have touched. It's not who we know that matters, but who we are inside other's heart.

Don't sit on two chairs because you'll just end up falling through the space between them. Decide on what you really want. Take your side not in betweens.

Worrying has never solved a problem, never paid a bill, and never cured an illness. Worrying is like racing a car engine in neutral gear. It doesn't get us anywhere and it uses gas. So let's stop worrying... all we need is a prayer and a heart full of FAITH.

Life is like a party... you invite a lot of people; some go, some join you, some didn't come... but in the end, after the fun, there would be few who would clean up the mess with you... and most of the time... those were the uninvited ones...

You deserve a day where worries don't get in the way. A day where, even if some people are insensitive or unkind, you're not going to mind because the blessings in your life are far, far better than the burdens.

When you share beautiful moments with those who become a part of your life, no matter how small, these become imprinted in their memories for a lifetime.

One thing worse than quitting is being afraid to begin... always remember that doing your best is more important than being the best.

Worries are like birds... let them fly over you but don't let them build a nest over your head. Life is beautiful... keep it worry – free.

Life is a mirror. What you see in others, is a reflection of what you see in yourself. Those who size up everyone they meet and point out their mistakes don't like themselves.

About the Author

Glen Quilab was a Leadership Trainer/Facilitator in a non-government organization for almost 7 years. He was known as a motivator, educator and encourages the youth leaders in his area to take the challenge and lead a fruitful life. He has conducted several leadership trainings in different areas in the Philippines and has facilitated a National Trainers Training for Leadership several times. He is awarded as one of the Top Ten Most Outstanding Red Cross Youth in 2004 in the Philippines.

www.ingramcontent.com/pod-product-compliance
Lightning Source LLC
Chambersburg PA
CBHW070248290526
45789CB00004B/1808